FOUNDATIONAL PRINCIPLES FOR NEW CONVERTS AND BELIEVERS

Augusto Perez

FOUNDATIONAL PRINCIPLES FOR NEW
CONVERTS AND BELIEVERS
ISBN 0-9678473-1-1

Copyright©2005 by Augusto L. Perez

All scripture references are taken from the
King James Version of the Bible.

Published by:
Augusto L. Perez

For information on bookings or to place an order
please contact us at:

The Appearance Ministries, Inc.
P.O. Box 465
Live Oak, FL. 32064
Web Address: www.theappearance.com
Email: augusto@theappearance.com

TABLE OF CONTENTS

1

YOUR NEW LIFE

Welcome to the kingdom of our Father! As a new creature in Christ Jesus you have just embarked upon the greatest adventure any human being can experience. Along with many millions of others throughout the world, you have been supernaturally born into God's eternal kingdom. Your faith in Jesus Christ as Lord, your obedience to His Word and your commitment to Him have brought about this wonderful event in your life. Big changes will begin to take place in your life that are difficult to understand. As you read on you will receive guidance and valuable information that will help you to mature and grow as a new believer.

A. Our Father's Kingdom

The kingdom of God is one of light, righteousness, holiness, blessing, love, joy, and peace. As you start to understand what has happened to you since you were born again, your heart will be filled with joy and gratitude toward our heavenly Father.

1. Born Into A New Realm

a. *Born of the Water (John 3:3-7; Acts 2:38) and of the Spirit (John 3:3-7; I Peter 1:23)*

Millions of people all over the world believe in God, and talk to Him in their own way, but have never really had an encounter with Him. They don't know Him *(John 5:37).* To them, God is a religion. They live a life

1

of sin and feel no conviction because they are dead in their trespasses and sins *(Ephesians 2:1-9; Colossians 2:13).*

After you are born again, you will never be the same again. Now, you have had a personal encounter with God, and because you have His life dwelling inside of you, everything will look different to you. The heavens, the trees, people will all look more beautiful and brilliant to you, because now you can see them without the veil of darkness and sin that was covering your eyes before. You will love everybody, regardless of color or race. Now when you read the Bible you will be able to understand it and identify with it. No longer is it a dull book that you dreaded to read.

Now, you can talk to Him as your father and very dear friend, and He will talk back to you. You will now be able to hear His voice because your spiritual ears have been circumcised. Your five physical senses have been quickened; therefore you can feel His presence and love in a very real way. As you go about your daily life, He is there with you. The reason you have such joy and peace is because you have just had an encounter with your creator, the God of all the earth. Only He can give you true joy and peace.

A great hunger will awaken in you to know God more and learn His Word. Now you will desire to talk about God and the things of God with everybody. You have a desire to share with everyone what has happened in your life. You will have a tremendous desire to go to church and be with other people of God. This is a sign that you have been born again.

2.   **Begotten Of The Father**

a.   Received Our Father's nature (Ezekiel 36:25-27; John 1:12; 2 Corinthians 5:17; I John 3:1-2;)

Because of God's nature inside of you, the bad things you used to do before, you don't do anymore. If you used to practice fornication, adultery, drunkenness, lying, stealing, cursing, you don't do that anymore. You feel repulsed and offended by it because the Holy Spirit of God dwells inside you. Does this mean that now you are perfect? Does it mean that you will never make mistakes? No, that is not what it means. You will commit sins, but you will not live a life of sin, practicing sins every day. If you commit a sin, you need to repent immediately and ask God to forgive *(I John 1:8-10)*.

Although your spirit has been born again, your soul (mind) needs to be renewed day by day. You still have habits, ways of thinking, traditions and lifestyle that will change as you are being transformed more and more into the image of Christ by prayer and reading of the Bible every day. You cannot change by yourself without the help of the Holy Spirit. Only He can change us. We will cover more about this further ahead.

b. Became the children of God (Romans 8:14-16)

After we are born again, God adopts you us a sons, and as a result, we are no longer just the creation of God, but sons of God. As sons we have rights, privileges, authority and power to use His name. We are now heirs of the riches of His kingdom which before we did not enjoy because they did not belong to us. Now we are able to enjoy all the promises of God found in the Bible because we are the children of God.

B. Your Father's House

When you are saved, God puts you in a local church, and gives you a pastor to guide you and help you grow spiritually. In time, you will learn to love him and trust his counsel. Every time there is a gathering of believers,

3

you need to make every attempt to be a part of it. The Lord expects you to be faithful and committed and serve Him in that Church. Let's take a look at God's House, what it is, what is in it and why it is so important in your life.

1. What Is It?
(Ephesians 2:19-22; I Peter 2:5; I Timothy 3:15

The Church is the House of the Lord, built upon the foundation of apostles and prophets, Jesus Christ Himself being the chief cornerstone. It is not an organization, but a living organism. When God's people come together in one building, it becomes a habitation of God through His Spirit, a place that houses the presence of Almighty God. The House of God!

As each believer, being a lively stone, a holy priest offering spiritual sacrifices acceptable to God by Jesus Christ, begins to worship God in spirit and in truth *(John 4:23)*, God manifests in their midst and receives their individual and collective spiritual sacrifices *(Romans 12:1-2)*.

2. What Is In It?

The house of God is where we go with other believers to receive instruction, training, discipleship, guidance, strength and fellowship. Every believer has gifts, talents and abilities given to them by God for the purpose of ministering and helping others. You should make a commitment to be in service as often as possible.

If a believer does not gather together with other believers in the house of God, he is depriving himself and others of a great blessing. When all the believers gather together in one church building, they are able to have fellowship with each other and the blood of Jesus washes them from all sins *(I John 1:7)*.

4

C. Growing Up In His House

Growing and maturing in the spiritual realm is pretty much as in the natural realm. Understand that no matter what your age may be, you were born as a baby into God's kingdom. The rate at which you grow in the spirit will depend on you. God ordained His house to help you grow and mature spiritually.

1. Growing-Up In The Lord

As a baby grows into a child and matures, it also grows in its ability to understand. Likewise, you too are a babe in the Spirit! You will gain a greater understanding of spiritual things, as you grow older in the Spirit. Your spiritual growth will depend not only on time, but also on your diligence in seeking to know your heavenly Father and His plans for your life. Getting to know Him better will build your confidence and security in His love for you.

The insecurities of an adopted child can be compared to how you feel as a newcomer to God's family! You have entered into new and unfamiliar surroundings and there is much adjusting to do. You brought with you a collection of memories, bad habits, experiences, and wrong ways of thinking. As God's adopted child, you'll undergo changes in your lifestyle, environment and ways of thinking.

2. Learning To Eat

You must start with the milk of God's word *(I Peter 2:2, 3:18; 2 Peter 3:18).* If you try to eat too much too soon, it will lead to spiritual indigestion and frustration. Be patient, He will feed you, as you are able to bear it. There has never been an infant that was able to stand on his weak, little legs and begin to walk right away. First they crawl, stand, stagger, stumble and even fall down a

5

few times before he is finally able to walk. In the realm of the spirit you are the same. It takes a long time to develop those spiritual muscles of faith. The more you feed on the word of God and pray, the faster you will grow and the stronger you will become. Develop a prayer closet where you pray to your heavenly father everyday, and develop intimacy with Him.

If you get too confident and try to move faster than your spiritual legs can carry you, you will get into trouble and fall and hurt yourself. On the other hand, if you don't have enough confidence and faith, you will take too long to take the first few steps. Learn to develop balance in everything you do. Do not get discouraged over the first few mistakes you make. We all make mistakes as we grow and develop, some more, some less but everyone makes their share of blunders. It's important that you understand that spiritual growth is a process that will take many years.

You must learn to develop patience, for it will be your best ally as you start to grow spiritually and mature. Enjoy these times of your new experience with the Lord. Just like the childhood years, they are magical and special and will never return. This is only the beginning of an exciting new life and adventure that is in store for you *(Ephesians 3:17-19)*. God loves you very much, and His family loves you too. Welcome into the family of our heavenly Father!

2

WHY YOU MUST BE BAPTIZED IN WATER

Now that you have received Jesus Christ as your Lord and Savior, you need to be baptized in water. In order to understand the meaning of water baptism correctly, we need to take a trip to the past, to the beginning when everything started. God created man on the earth because He wanted to have communion with him. When Adam sinned, his relationship with God was broken. After this, God dealt with man through covenants He made with righteous men that were confirmed through signs.

The rainbow was a sign of the covenant between man and God indicating that God would never again destroy the world by water. However, God searched for a man with whom He could make a more intimate and lasting covenant. In Ur of the Chaldees God found such a man: Abraham, the first human being with whom He made a *Covenant of Relationship....*

A. The Circumcision

The circumcision was a covenant through which man would put a mark in his own body indicating that he was separated unto God and that he belonged to God *(Genesis 17:9-14)*. This was an unbreakable blood covenant that made the Jewish people different to any other group of people in the world. Even when God decided to destroy Sodom and Gomorrah, He considered the covenant He had made with His servant Abraham and consulted with him first.

This covenant was practiced by all the descendants of Abraham until God made another covenant with the Jews on Mount Sinai, the *Ten Commandments* (*Exodus 24:7-8, Daniel 9:4, Nehemiah 1:5, Psalms 195:8-9*). Under the Old Covenant made with Abraham and later with Moses, the Jews had to shed the blood of animals in sacrifices and do the rite of circumcision to enter into a covenant with God. This continued until the coming of the Lamb of God, Jesus Christ who established a New Covenant with His twelve apostles (*John 1:29, Mathew 26:26-29, Daniel 9:27*).

B.   The New Covenant

After the *New Covenant* was instituted, the blood of animals in sacrifices and circumcision were not necessary anymore. That's why the early church abolished those rites for the believers **(Acts 15)**. To enter into a New Covenant with God, a new rite of initiation is required, different to the others. This *New Covenant* was established by the Lord Jesus Christ through His death, burial and resurrection **(Luke 22:19, Hebrews 9:15)**.

What is the rite of initiation to enter into the *New Covenant?* In order to enter into a New Covenant with God we must become partaker of the death (repentance), burial (water baptism), and resurrection (Holy Spirit) of the Lord Jesus Christ *(Acts 2:38, Romans 6:3-4, Luke 3:16-17)*. While natural Israel had to be circumcised in the flesh, and blood was shed when a cut was made into the flesh, those who are born again today (spiritual Israel) are circumcised in the heart (*heart surgery*). Without this operation in the heart, man is incapable of loving God. The sinful nature, the enmity against God is removed and replaced by a love for God. You are changed in the very depths of your heart. You now desire to obey and please God and can truly worship Him from your heart.

8

Can any person be considered a member of the Church of Jesus Christ if he has not been baptized in water? Not more than any Jew could enter into the Old Covenant without being circumcised. What happened in Samaria when Phillip preached the gospel? *(Acts 8:12)*. What was the eunuch's answer when he heard Phillip's preaching? *(Acts 8:36-38)*. How was the apostle Paul initiated to the church by Ananias? *(Acts 22:16)*.

C. The Baptism in Water

The baptism in water is a sacred covenant instituted by Jesus Christ through which we are baptized into Christ and into His death. Baptism takes the place of the rite of circumcision of the Old Covenant. *(Mathew 28:18-20, Romans 6:3-7)*.

The Greek word for baptism means to *submerge, cover completely*. It is obvious from these descriptions that those that were baptized in the early church in the book of Acts, were immersed in water. There are two extreme sets of beliefs today in reference to water baptism. One says that if a person is not baptized, he is not saved. The other one does not place much emphasis in water baptism saying it does not matter. *Both are incorrect.* The Bible teaches us that salvation is by grace (you cannot do anything to earn it), through faith; and even faith you have, is a gift from God. Not by works so that no one may glory in it. *(Ephesians 2:8-9, Romans 3:24, 4:16, 5:2, 11:6)*.

In the book of *Romans 4:1-12* we can read that *Abraham was justified before God by faith, not by anything he did.* In *verses 10-11* we also read that Abraham obtained righteousness before God through his faith, when he was not yet circumcised. He received the circumcision afterward as a sign, a seal of righteousness of the faith that he had obtained when he was yet uncircumcised. In Other words, Abraham was justified before God through his faith, and he was circumcised years later as a sign, a seal of that righteousness that he had already received before through his faith.

Likewise, when a person believes in the redemptive work of Jesus Christ and repents, he is forgiven of all his sins and justified before God. Nevertheless, such a person must be baptized in water after his conversion as a sign, a seal of the righteousness that he received before from God through his faith. Many believers have been filled with the Holy Spirit when they heard and believed the gospel by faith before they were baptized in water. In *Acts 10:44-48* we read how Cornelius and all his house received the Holy Spirit when they heard Peter share with them the gospel of Jesus Christ. Afterwards, Peter commanded them to be baptized in the name of the Lord Jesus Christ.

In my own experience I have seen many people filled with the Holy Spirit and speaking in other tongues when they heard the gospel of salvation, and then consequently were baptized. Every person that confesses Jesus Christ as their savior and repents of his sins must be baptized in water to enter the New Covenant that Jesus established through His blood, and be called a Christian.

When our hearts are circumcised, God puts His seal of righteousness over us, making us the heirs of all the promises of Abraham. While in the Old Testament the Jews were circumcised in the flesh, in the New Covenant the circumcision is in the heart, through the Holy Spirit. The enmity against God and our corruptible nature is removed and replaced by a love for God *(Deuteronomy 30:6; Colossians 1:12-14; 2:11-12 and Romans 2:28-29, 5:10, 6:16).* Our own nature is changed. Now we don't resist the Holy Sprit, but are free to obey Him and please Him from our hearts. The Bible teaches us that when we are circumcised in our hearts, the Holy Spirit immerses us in Christ and gives us His nature, making us members of His body, the Church *(1 Corinthians 12:13; Romans 2:28-29; Galatians 3:27).*

When a person is born again of the water (baptism in water) and the spirit, there is a transformation in the spirit of the person that is the same as a second birth, and the old Adamic nature is removed and replaced by the nature of Christ. This is what is commonly known as *Born Again* **(John 3:5-7).** Without this change in the heart, man can't love God or have an intimate relationship with Him *(Ezekiel 11:19-20, 1 Peter 3:21; 2 Peter 1:2-4).*

D. What Happens At Baptism?

When a person is baptized in water, he is identified with the death, burial and resurrection of Jesus Christ that He experienced in our place, and the *enmity against God* that was in us due to original sin (the corruption of our fallen nature, spiritual blindness and death), is removed. At baptism we are circumcised in our hearts (heart surgery) so that we are free to love God and able to have fellowship with Him. We are initiated into the *New Covenant* and become the property of God. This makes us accountable to Him for how we live our lives, but also as part of the New Covenant, we have the right to all the benefits and promises contained in the Bible.

Everyone that believes and confesses that Jesus is the Christ needs to be baptized in water. To be able to be baptized in water, there must be evidence of genuine repentance of sins and faith in the redemptive work of Jesus Christ *(Mark 16:16; John 3:5; Romans 6:5; Acts 8:36-38).* Children should only be baptized when the Holy Spirit has revealed Jesus Christ in their hearts, and they have fully understood the meaning of baptism in water. *Babies must not be baptized.* Baptism in water is only for believers that have repented of their sins and understood the gospel. A baby does not have the faculty of understanding the gospel and repenting. People have to believe and then be baptized, not the other way around *(Mark 16:16; Acts 2:38).*

E. How Should I Be Baptized?

Baptism in water must be by immersion, and it must be done in the name of the Triune God, the *Lord Jesus Christ.* That is the name of the *Triune God. Lord* (the *JHVH* of the Old Testament), *Jesus* (the earthly, human name, son of God), and *Christ* (the name of the Holy Spirit, the anointing, the Messiah). The apostles obeyed the Lord and baptized all the believers in this manner *(Mathew 28:19; Acts 8:14-16; 10:48; 19:1-5; 22:16; Philippians 2:9; Colossians 3:17).*

It is possible to be baptized in water and not be circumcised in the heart if the believer did not prepare himself adequately. When this happens, baptism becomes just a religious ritual where someone goes in dry and comes out wet, and not a real, personal experience. If you have been baptized in the past but you do not feel that you have had a genuine experience in your heart, or you were baptized when you were a baby, pray to God and ask the Holy Spirit to show you what you must do. If you feel the Lord is guiding you to be baptized again, obey Him and be re-baptized. Water baptism is a commandment from the Lord that must be obeyed *(Ephesians 4:4-5; 1 Corinthians 12:13).*

3

THE BAPTISM OF THE HOLY SPIRIT

Because God is supernatural, transcending the natural realm, we cannot truly come to know Him and understand Him unless we move into the realm of the spirit. We can only truly worship God in the spirit because He is a spirit *(John 4:24)*. For some inexplicable reason the Lord has chosen us, puny and weak earthen vessels, to manifest His glory and power on the earth. It is not that He could not do it Himself, or have His holy angels sent to accomplish whatever mission He needed done. The Lord simply delights in sharing His glory with His creation, and using us as partners to achieve His pre-ordained divine plans. Therefore it behooves us to learn and understand His ways, kingdom and how He desires to reveal His power and glory through us.

In **1 Corinthians 4:20** Paul said: *"the kingdom of God does not consist in words, but in power."* The Holy Spirit is the inner power that God gives us to help us to live in this world, while we are pilgrims here. None of us is worthy to have the Spirit of God living in us in this manner, but we must understand that it is by the righteousness of Christ that we are accepted by God. Our focus must always be who He is in us, and not who we are in our own strength, ability and intellect. No one deserves this gift from God or has ever done anything to earn it. For it is only by grace, through faith that we receive it *(Ephesians 2:8-9)*.

If our goal is to become like Jesus, then we must look beyond our own weaknesses and inabilities, and rise above the terrestrial so we can enjoy the celestial. We must move into the invisible, eternal realm to be able to flow and operate in the realm of the supernatural *(2 Corinthians 4:18)*. Our intimate relationship with the Lord is directly proportional to the amount of the power of His Spirit that will flow through us. But the door that we must all go through to step into the invisible, supernatural realm of God's kingdom is the baptism in the Holy Spirit.

Through the Holy Spirit, God pours His love into our hearts *(Romans 5:5)*. This love is not like any human love we have ever experienced or felt. This love transcends the human and elevates us into the divine. As we are filled with this liquid love, it begins to transform us and manifest God's love through us to others *(1 John 4:7-13)*. This is the kind of love that loves the unlovable, the undeserving and those that hate you and despitefully use you. When you have this kind of love, you are able to forgive anyone, anything they may have done unto you. Let's take a look at this wonderful experience and how you can receive it in your Christian life.

A.   What Is The Baptism Of The Holy Spirit?

This is a topic that causes much confusion and contention in the body of Christ. I thank the Lord that He allowed me to have the glorious experience of the baptism of the Holy Spirit the same night that I was baptized in water in a Pentecostal Church twenty four years ago. However, I noticed through the years that not all believers had that same experience. I saw many that although they had repented and been baptized in water, had not been able to speak with tongues. These believers had a genuine conversion, loved the Lord, lived godly lives, yet in spite of their tears, fasts and continuous repentance, they were not able to speak with tongues.

The doctrine of the church to which I belonged believed that if a believer did not speak in tongues, he had not received the Holy Spirit, and therefore had not been born again. It took me several years of God dealing with me, revealing His word to me to be able to understand how wrong they were. Every one that has been born again has the Holy Spirit dwelling inside. *"If a man has not the spirit of Christ, he is none of His" (Romans 8:9).* Other groups also have doctrinal errors although maybe not as extreme. Many Christians believe that there is nothing more after accepting Jesus as their Lord and Savior and being baptized in water, which is not true. *Many believe that the baptism of the Spirit, spiritual gifts, signs and wonders, apostles and prophets are not for today.* Some even attribute speaking in tongues to the devil, which is a very dangerous accusation, since they are in danger of committing the unpardonable sin and can be punished severely *(Mathew 12:31-32, Mark 3:28-30, 1 Timothy 1:13, Hebrews 10:26).*

There is a difference between having the Spirit and being baptized in the Spirit. When someone is saved by believing with the heart and confessing with his mouth that Jesus died for his sins, he receives the incorruptible seed of God's Spirit in his innermost being *(1 Peter 1:23).* That person can then be filled with the Spirit that is already dwelling inside him if he believes and receives with faith *(John 7:37-39).* Even in the life of our Lord Jesus Christ, He did not do any mighty works until He was baptized with the Holy Spirit at the river Jordan *(Mathew 3:16-17).* Although Jesus was God manifested in the flesh, it was necessary for Him to be empowered by the Spirit. The early church disciples also were commanded by the Lord to wait in the upper room until they were filled with power from on high *(Luke 24:49).*

On the day of Pentecost in *Acts 2*, the apostles received a double experience. First they received the Holy Spirit Jesus sent from heaven, and at the same time they were baptized in the Spirit to be able to do the work of the ministry that Jesus had commanded them. As a result, they spoke in tongues and had many other powerful manifestations of the Spirit. Three thousand were added to the Church that same day, but the Bible does not say if they were all filled with the Spirit.

15

In *Acts 4:31* it says that the apostles were filled with the Holy Spirit. If salvation and being filled with the Spirit is the same thing, then the apostles were saved again for a second time in *Acts 4.* In *1 Corinthians 12:13* Paul said: *"For we were baptized by one same spirit into the Body".* This scripture tells us clearly that the way to enter into the Body of Christ (the church) is through the Holy Spirit in the new birth experience. *The baptism of the Holy Spirit with the evidence of speaking in new tongues is different to the new birth experience. Speaking in tongues has to do with the infilling of the Holy Spirit. Paul said: "We all have been baptized into one Body and made to drink of one spirit* (*1 Corinthians 12:13*).

When someone who is saved, is thirsty and opens up to the Holy Spirit drinking from Him, he is filled or possessed with the Spirit of God that already lives within him *(John 7:37-39, Galatians 4:6-7).* Thousands of believers have a misunderstanding of what the baptism of the Holy Spirit is and spend years praying for God to give them this experience. They do not know that the Holy Spirit is already inside them and they only have to desire and allow the Spirit to fill and baptize them.

B.   Who Can Be Filled With The Holy Spirit?

Although the baptism of the Holy Spirit and speaking in tongues are not a requirement to be saved, the will of God is that everyone be filled with His Spirit *(Ephesians 5:18).* It is so important that the last words of Jesus before He went up to heaven were about this theme *(Acts 1:4-9).* The apostle Peter full of the Holy Spirit on the day of Pentecost confirmed it *(Acts 2:38).* That's how the early apostolic church started and continued afterward as well *(Acts 2:42).*

In these last days, the Lord is taking the church to its primitive roots, the apostolic foundation, to the doctrines the spiritual fathers established in the church. To be filled with the Holy Spirit is a right and a privilege for every believer. They received the Holy Spirit in Samaria *(Acts 8:14-20)*, in Caesarea *(Acts 10:44-48)* and in Ephesus *(Acts 19:1-7)*. Without a doubt, everyone that believed on the Lord Jesus Christ in the early Apostolic Church was baptized in water by immersion and filled with the Holy Spirit with the evidence of speaking in other tongues. This promised experience is for everyone today, for whomsoever the Lord shall call *(Acts 2:39)*.

C. The Evidence

When we read the Bible, it is evident that every time someone received the Holy Spirit there was evidence, an external sign that could not be denied. No one ever received the baptism of the Holy Spirit in secret, without someone who is near finding out. In Jerusalem a group of Jews saw it and heard it *(Acts 8:18)*, and in Caesarea, the ones that were with Peter heard it too *(Acts 10:46)*.

What was it that the people saw and heard? When the Spirit fell the first time in the upper room, there was wind, fire and tongues. But the other manifestations that took place after this initial outpouring did not come with fire nor wind, but only tongues were heard as the Spirit gave them to speak *(Acts 11:15)*. In the city of Ephesus Paul asked the people if they had received the Holy Spirit after they had believed. When they said no, Paul laid hands on them and they received the Holy Spirit with the evidence of speaking in other tongues. Paul did not ask them again if they had received the baptism of the Holy Spirit because he heard them himself speaking in tongues and praising God in angelic tongues *(Acts 19:1-7)*.

The evidence is that when a believer receives the baptism of the Holy Spirit, he speaks in tongues as a sign that he has received it. It is not the only sign, but it is the most prevalent one throughout the Bible that a believer has been baptized in the Spirit. However, there are many

Christians that have never been baptized in the Spirit and have never spoken in tongues *(1 Corinthians 12:30).*

Why tongues? The tongue can be used to bless or curse. It is the only member of our body that can corrupt the whole body. It is untamable, full of poison and evil *(James 3:8).* Man can control a horse with bit and bridle and can guide a ship with a rudder; however he cannot tame the tongue. Jesus mentioned tongues as one of the signs that would follow believers *(Mark 16:17).* When the Holy Spirit enters and fills the heart of a person, God reclaims possession of a person's tongue *(Isaiah 28:11).* He wants to possess our hearts, minds, bodies, desires and our tongues. *Some people want to receive the baptism of the Holy Spirit, but do not want to speak in tongues.* Paul says in the Bible that he wished everyone spoke in tongues, and that he spoke in tongues more than they did; and told them not to forbid speaking in tongues *(1 Corinthians 14:5, 18, 39).*

D. How Do You Receive the Baptism of the Holy Spirit?

Let's take a look at some important steps to receive this wonderful experience of the baptism of the Spirit.

1. *There Must Be Genuine Repentance (Acts 2:38)*

Repentance is to turn 180 degrees from the direction where we were heading and start walking to God, allowing Him to be the Lord of our lives. The moment you sincerely repent, God will forgive you immediately and you will feel as though a great weight has been lifted from your soul. Now you can talk to God and ask Him to fill you with His Holy Spirit, which you may receive right there and then, but there is second necessary step.

2. You Need to be Baptized in Water

In repentance you die to a life of sin, and in water baptism you are buried *(see chapter 2)*. When you come out of the water, it is symbolic of your resurrection to newness of life and God can then fill you with His Holy Spirit at the moment of baptism, while you are still in the water. God does not always move in the same way. Some receive the Holy Spirit before they are baptized in water, others afterwards *(Acts 10:44-48)*. The important thing is to be obedient to His commandment *(Acts 5:32)*.

3. Offer Him Sincere Worship from the Heart

Worship is not the same as giving thanks to God in prayer. It is something that maybe you are not used to doing, especially if you are a man. Do not be nervous, tense or fearful, it will only make it more difficult to receive the gift from God. Feel relaxed, comfortable, with confidence to receive what the Lord wants to give you. Think about Jesus with His arms stretched towards you. Raise your hands to Him as if you were going to embrace Him, and start to worship Him with expressions like: Alleluia! Glory! *With worship that comes out of your innermost being, not from your mind.*

God loves this kind of worship in spirit and in truth *(John 4:23-24)*. After all, is that not what you always have desired; to love God in spirit and in truth, without any barriers or obstacles; to be in him and him in you, in an inexplicable spiritual ecstasy? *(1 Peter 1:8)*.

4. Have Faith That He Will Fulfill What He Promised

God is not going to give you something that is not good, something that can harm you. If men being evil know how to give good gifts to their children, how much more will our heavenly father give the Holy Spirit to them that ask Him? *(Luke 11:9-13).* Ask with faith, confidence and insistence and you will receive living waters from God. You have already obeyed the Word, done your part, now God will do His part, you only have to receive. Proceed to make contact with God, where you are going to feel His divine presence. A warmth will touch your heart, and possibly you will be surprised when you feel hot tears running down your cheeks, while you speak words of love and gratitude for his forgiveness and great love for you *(John 3:16).*

5.   *Let the Holy Spirit Immerse You*

When you feel the presence of the Lord no dot stop, but continue to worship Him. Warmth will touch your heart. You have to leave the dimension of human thought and cross to the dimension of the Holy Spirit. God's ways are not our ways *(Isaiah 55:9).* Your attitude has to be like that of a child *(Mathew 18:3),* and confide in Him one hundred percent.   Like a child believes and obeys, so likewise you start a spiritual transformation. You will find yourself sinking more and more into the ocean of God's love.   Your lips will start to shake, and tears will start to run down your cheeks, your voice will intensify. Stretch your hands like a child towards the strong arms of your Heavenly Father.   Talking about the baptism of the Spirit Jesus said: *If anyone thirsts, come to me and drink; he that believes in me, as the scripture says, out of his belly shall flow living waters" (John 7:37-39).*

6.   *Drink of the Living Water Jesus is Giving you to Drink*

No one can drink with his mouth closed.   God says: "Open your mouth and I will fill it." God cannot fill your mouth if it is closed.   Some people do not receive the infilling of the Holy Spirit because they close their mouths, or do not open them enough. *Open your mouth with confidence and let the Lord fill it with angelic words that He will put in your heart.* You are thirsty for that living water, receive it. Thirst is one of man's most urgent needs and can be quenched with water or with some other beverage. But the thirst of the soul can only be quenched with the water that proceeds from heaven *(Isaiah 55:1; 44:3; Revelation 21:6, 22:17).*

If you try to quench the thirst of your soul with things of this world, you will realize that your spiritual thirst will not be quenched *(Job 29:23).* You can be surrounded with water, but you will die of thirst unless you open your mouth and drink. In the New Testament, the word spirit also means breath. Breathe deeply this breath of God and you will speak freely the words that He is giving you to speak.

7. Give the Control of Your Tongue to the Lord.

On the day of Pentecost, everyone started to speak in other tongues as the spirit gave them utterance *(Acts 2:4).* The same way a teacher shows the students how to say a poem, she does not say the poem, but only shows them what they must say. The same way, the Holy Spirit does not force anyone to speak in tongues, nor does it speak through anyone as if they were phonographs. *What the Spirit does is guide, giving us words or suggesting what we should say. It is not begging or persuading.*

The disciples on the day of Pentecost spoke the words the Spirit suggested to them, but it was them who spoke voluntarily. They did not care how strange the words were going to sound, nor what the people thought; *they just spoke in faith whatever the Spirit gave them to speak.* Not everyone speaks the same when they are filled with the Holy Spirit; some speak in a low voice, others scream, but it always starts with short words of one syllable. While those words are there, say them again and again until He gives you more to say. While you are receiving, He will continue to give you more.

Just like children do not speak great words at first, but start by saying simple words like "dada"; it is the same when you start to speak in tongues. You are starting to form words with your lips and tongue. This is the way every person starts to speak naturally and supernaturally, in our own native tongue and also in the tongue of angels *(1 Corinthians 13:1).* Someone helped us, encouraged us, syllable by syllable, word by word, phrase by phrase. Our Heavenly Father is pleased as any human father would be, when you start to say words in the language of the spirit He wants to hear. Can't you hear His voice encouraging you: *"Speak my child, speak."*

E. The Pentecostal Language

The Holy Spirit will prompt you to express yourself in the following ways:

1. *Stammering Lips (Isaiah 28:11)*

This happens when your lips and tongue start to shake. If this happens, speak clearly in faith. This is a sign that there is another tongue present. This is where many people stop the Holy Spirit from manifesting, because they insist in speaking in their own language when He is guiding us to speak in His language. You will continue to stammer as long as you persist in speaking in your own native tongue. When you start to babble and stutter, immediately stop trying to speak in your own language and start to speak in the unknown tongue. *You cannot speak two languages at the same time. It is not possible.* When you feel that God is present to baptize you, do not hinder the Lord by repeating words or phrases in your known language.

Sometimes while the Spirit is trying to lead a person to speak in other tongues, because of the blessing the person is experiencing, they start to say: "Glory, glory, glory" never allowing the Holy Spirit to baptize them. When the Holy Spirit comes upon you to baptize you, *do not say anything in your own tongue, but say the words and sounds He is giving you to say.* Do not drown them in your unbelief.

When you feel the words of the Spirit inside of you, you will feel an urge to say them. This may happen when you are praying, reading the Bible or just worshipping the Lord. When you feel the urge to say these words, do not reject them, obey Him and you will speak in tongues. Some people expect the Spirit to do everything, or think these urges are from the flesh. But the flesh will never lead anyone to the baptism of the Holy Spirit *(Galatians 5:17).* The flesh is opposed to tongues. It will tell you that it is you who are inventing the words, or you are just repeating what you heard someone else say. The flesh wants to express itself and cause you to continue to speak in your native tongue, and not in angelic tongues.

2. *Strange Sounds and Words*

The Bible tells us that the Holy Spirit is the one that initiates speaking in tongues. Those sounds and words do not come from your flesh or your imagination, the Holy Spirit is giving them to you. Some people have even seen themselves in dream speaking in tongues, and when they woke up they simply continued speaking in tongues.

When you feel the presence of the Holy Spirit, simply continue the internal impulses and start to speak in tongues without knowing what you will say. It is an act of faith *(Hebrews 11:8).* The key word is to *trust in God.* Without knowing exactly what you will say, you allow God to guide you while you are speaking. Do not doubt; prepare yourself to speak in tongues when God fills you with the Holy Spirit. God is giving you words to say, do it with confidence and faith.

The Holy Spirit has already been given. God does not have anything else to give; it is you who has to receive. Receive it confidently, simply and calmly. Do not be nervous or rigid; do not doubt or resist it, but simply open your mouth and drink the living waters He is giving you. Speak those strange sounds that are coming from your heart, say them again and again and you will start to feel the bubbling sensations starting in the pit of your stomach as you are being filled with His Spirit. Continue to drink and don't stop until you are satisfied.

F. After Your Pentecost

This is what you have waited for and desired all your life. Your spirit has united to His. What a joy to know that He has filled you with His presence, and you are now the temple of the Holy Spirit. Thank and worship Him every day for giving you His precious Holy Spirit. Once you have been filled with the Spirit, do not remain there but renew your experience daily by drinking the living waters and letting Him fill you again and again. When the living waters are flowing inside of you, you will start to speak in tongues again. Each refilling can be more glorious that the original baptism.

When the believers are not directed to these new outpourings of the Spirit and to win others to the Lord, gradually they start to dry spiritually. Tell others about the experience you just had with the Lord, and watch how God will use you to touch many lives for His glory. One of the reasons you were baptized with the Spirit is to be a witness for Christ and to win others to the Lord. Your spiritual growth is very important, and to achieve that spiritual growth you need to pray, fast, read your Bible and attend a local church where you will be taught the word of God and how to live a Christian life.

4

HIDING THE WORD IN YOUR HEART

The Bible is not just any book, but it is a supernatural book, containing the living, incorruptible seed of the Word of God that is able to impart life to whosoever reads it. Thus the Bible cannot be read like any other book, but has to be read with the help and the leading of the Holy Spirit. The author of the Bible is not a man, but a supernatural God. The reason God gave us the Bible is because He wants to reveal Himself, His character and nature to us through its pages. There are little challenges throughout the Bible daring us to seek Him and to know Him in an intimate, personal way.

We need to learn to hide the Word of God in our hearts because it will help us to control our thoughts *(Proverbs 23:7; Philippians 4:8)* and to overcome sin *(Psalms 119:11)*. There are several methods to accomplish this. We should be careful to practice each one of the methods; otherwise, our relationship with the scriptures will be incomplete, like a puzzle with a missing piece. As you meditate and memorize the word of God it will hide in our hearts and it will come alive *(Psalm 1:1-2, 119:11)*.

The Bible is the greatest book in the world. It does not just contain the words of God; *it is the Word of God.* It contains many love letters from God to man. It also contains instruction for living, stories about love, adventure, war and mystery. If we are going to really get to know Him, we must get to know the book that reveals Him. We can never really love God more than we can obey Him, and can never really obey Him more than we can obey His word.

A. The Bible: God's Word

The Bible is no ordinary book. It was inspired by the Holy Spirit and therefore has the ability to impart life to those that read it. It is a very unique book because God is its author. Men who listened to the voice of God wrote the Bible. It has authority and power to change people's lives if they hearken to it *(Hebrews 4:12; 2 Timothy 3:15-16)*.

1. The Bible's History

The Bible was written over a 2,000 year span, by more than 40 writers from diverse walks of life: kings, prophets, peasants, shepherds, soldiers, fishermen, poets, apostles, scholars, doctors and others. It was written on three continents: Asia, Africa and Europe, and in three languages: Hebrew, Greek and Aramaic. Yet, it contains in its pages the same story: God's plan of salvation for humanity *(II Peter 1:20-21)*.

The Bible has survived centuries of persecution, criticisms and ridicule. It has not only survived, but it has become the most read book in the entire world and the all-time bestseller. The French atheist Voltaire said the Bible would be extinct by 1850. Voltaire is come and gone, and the Bible is still here. Not only that, but the home of Voltaire became a printing shop where Bibles were printed for many years *(Matthew 24:35)*.

2. The Bible's Reliability

No other book in the world can claim the Bible's accuracy of facts and prophecy. It predicted with incredible accuracy the futures of nations, races, cities and peoples. It gave incredible details about the coming of the Messiah. There are over 300 prophecies in the Old Testament alone, given from 1600 to 400 in advance concerning Messiah, predicting the birth, life, death and resurrection of the Lord Jesus Christ. The Bible has a total of 66 books and is divided into 2 parts: The Old Testament (39 books), and the New Testament (27 books). The word testament means *covenant*.

B. The Benefits of Reading the Bible

Reading the Word of God has incredible benefits and blessings. It will help you grow in the Lord. You should start by reading the four gospels of Mathew, Mark, Luke and John. Meditate on what you read and try to apply it to your life. Following is a list of some of the things we receive when we read the Bible:

1. Salvation

The Bible has a message of good news, the gospel of salvation. It has the road map to Heaven that tells you what you must do in order to go there *(I Peter 1:23-25)*.

2. Faith

We received salvation by grace through faith and it is important to continue to walk with God by faith. The Bible says that without faith it is impossible to please God *(Hebrews 11:6)*. Our walk with God is dependent on our faith and trust in Him *(II Corinthians 5:7)*. How do we get it? *(Romans 10:17)*.

3. Nourishment

The Word of God is food for our souls. We can't live by natural bread alone *(Job 23:12)*. The Word is described in the Bible as milk *(I Peter 2:2)*, honey *(Psalm 119:103)*, bread *(Luke 4:4)*, water *(Ephesians 5:26)* and meat, *(I Corinthians 3:2; Hebrews 5:12-14))*.

4. Guidance

His Word guides us in our walk through life, and helps us find the will of God for us *(Psalms 119:105)*.

5. Peace

The best way to receive peace when we go through times of trouble, fear and turmoil is by reading His Word *(Isaiah 26:3; Psalms 119:165)*.

C. The Benefits of Hearing the Word of God

Hearing the Word being preached and taught by anointed men and women of God will produce faith in you *(Romans 10:17; Revelation 1:3).* Just because you hear something preached, or read it in some Christian book does not mean it is necessarily true. Search the scriptures to make sure the Bible backs it up before you accept and embrace anything *(Acts 17:11)*. If you are still confused, ask your pastor and other men of God who are wise and experienced.

Christian music will also minister to you and bless you. Thanks to present day technology, we can hear the Word of God and Christian music in the form of cassettes, CD's, videotapes and Christian TV Programs. You can listen to the word of God while you are driving in your car, walking, jogging or just doing work around the house. Try to saturate your life with God's word everyday as much as possible. It will help you grow and develop into a strong Christian.

We have Christian Rap CD's that are loaded with the word of God, and each song is like a small message in itself. We also have other resource materials that will help you grow strong in the Lord. For more information you may visit our website at www.theappearance.com.

5

LEARNING HOW TO PRAY

Prayer is the greatest privilege we have as the children of God. Man has always longed to talk to God, but did you know that our heavenly Father longs to talk with us and have intimate fellowship with us? Prayer should be as natural as breathing and as enjoyable as eating. God's heart is hungry for companionship with His children. His heart hunger is the reason for man and the reason for redemption. Of all things, what do you think the disciples of Jesus asked Him to teach them? They asked Him to teach then how to pray. Let's take a look at some principles of prayer.

A. What Is Prayer?

Prayer is our heavenly Father's invitation to visit with Him. Everything we are and have is because of Him. So prayer is simply talking it over with Him, getting His views, His plans, will, and carrying out these plans with His grace, ability and wisdom. It means that we are welcome to the Throne Room of Love. It is sons visiting their Father. It is children coming into the presence of a loving Father. Prayer keeps man in close contact with the Father and it enriches one spiritually. Prayer illuminates the mind, refreshes and heals the body and energizes our spirit. Prayer is a spiritual exercise; it is our spirit contacting the Father. But first, *you must choose to pray.*

B. Develop a Prayer Life

We are children of choice, and we are what we make ourselves. This prayer habit will be born of your own will. This habit is very hard for most people to form. However, it should never be a duty, for just like we don't enjoy those that visit us out of duty, so does our Heavenly Father *(Mathew 6:5)*. We want those who love us to come be with us because they enjoy it and want to. We should think of prayer as a rare opportunity and a great honor to meet with the God of the universe. However, there are some practical guidelines to follow if you are going to maintain an active prayer life.

1. Find a Time

You have chosen to pray; now you must find a time when to pray. David said, "Evening, morning and noon will I pray." Your prayer must be organized; the Lord is not opposed to order *(I Cor. 14:40)*. Few people succeed in praying unless you have a planned time set aside to pray. In finding the best time for daily prayer, give consideration to your personal life style. Don't try to do like someone else.

2. Find A Place

It helps if you establish in your home a place of prayer. *Luke 11:1* mentions that the Lord was praying in a certain place. Try to find a secret place, a *(closet)* place where you can get alone with God. In the Bible, prayer was done in a number of places: at a well, in open fields, in chains, in the belly of a fish, standing in a river, at a grave, on a cross, in a dungeon, in a shipwreck. So you see, where you pray is not important, as long as you pray.

C. Blueprint For Prayer

Jesus referred to an hour of prayer *(Mat. 26:40)*. His disciples asked Jesus how to pray. He answered it by teaching them the following prayer:

1. Our Father Who Is In Heaven

You acknowledge Him as your heavenly Father, and you thank Him for saving and making you His adopted son, and for all His blessings upon your life.

2. Hallowed Be Your Name

You worship His name, the name that is above every name "Jesus". Whenever you pray, you must pray to our heavenly father in the name of Jesus. That is the name that is above every name, in heaven, on earth and under the earth *(Acts 4:12; Philippians 2:9-11)*. That is the covenant name, and it has power and authority to save, heal, and deliver *(Mark 16:15-16)*. All that we do must be done in the name of Jesus because it is the only name recognized by God in Heaven *(Colossians 3:17)*. Then you can worship Him for the attributes of each of Bible names (Ex. Jehovah-rohe, Jehova-rapha etc.).

3. Your Kingdom Come

This is where you pray for His Kingdom, which is within you *(Luke 17:20-21)*, to be manifested in your life, home, family, church, city, country and the world. The Kingdom of God is righteousness, peace and joy in the Holy Spirit *(Romans 14:17)*.

31

4. Your Will Be Done On Earth As It Is In Heaven

What is the will of God? The general will of God is found in His Word. You need to know that, as well as what His specific will is and then you can pray this upon you situation, family, church, city, nation etc. This is a good place to hear from God.

5. Give Us This Day Our Daily Bread

In this part of your prayer, you may ask your Father for your personal needs. Feel confident to pray in faith for your personal needs, Jesus wants you to *(Matthew 7:7)*. If we pray according to His will, we should not pray with fear but with faith, believing that He will hear us and grant us what we are asking Him *(I John 5:14-15; Hebrews 11:6)*.

6. Forgive Us Our Sins

This is the part when we confess our sins and ask God to forgive us. Ask God to search your heart and show you any sins that you may not be aware of, but are still there like pride, unbelief, lust and un-forgiveness *(Psalms 139:23-24)*.

7. As We Forgive Those Who Sin Against Us

When we have something against someone in our heart, God does not hear our prayer. If we want God to hear our prayers and forgive us of our sins, we must be willing to forgive others who have hurt and offended us *(Mark 11:25-26)*. To forgive is to release someone who has hurt us, to cancel the debt that they owe us *(Mathew 18:21-35)*. You cannot wait to feel like forgiving someone, but you must will to forgive.

To forgive is not an alternative, but a command from the Lord. Un-forgiveness is a trap from the enemy to bring you into captivity and bondage. When you refuse to forgive someone, you are hurting yourself, not them. It does not matter how many years ago something happened, if you have not forgiven them, the root of bitterness is still there in your heart, defiling you *(Hebrews 12:14-15)*.

Make a list of all the people who have hurt you and forgive them from your heart, verbally expressing your forgiveness towards them. As you forgive, renounce all spirit of resentment, bitterness and hatred that may be in your heart. Ask God to forgive you for keeping all this un-forgiveness in your heart for all this time. If you blamed God for things that happened in you life, ask Him to forgive you. Also forgive yourself for all the mistakes you made, the Lord did *(Psalm 103:8-17)*.

8. Lead Us Not Into Temptation

Now that you are born again Christian, you must make an attempt to avoid places and people that are a sort of temptation to you. One of the hardest things for a new convert is to try to stay away from friends they used to hang around with who were a source of temptation to them. These people may want you to continue to do those things with them, but now you are a different person and they may not be able understand that *(I Peter 4:1-4)*.

Many new converts think they are strong enough to be able to hang around with their old buddies so they can win them to the Lord. But this strategy usually backfires. In time, when you are older in the things of God, you may be able to become friends and hang around with some sinners out there in order to win them to the Lord.

I strongly recommend that in the beginning of your conversion, you do not hang around with them in the hope of winning them to Christ. You are still not strong enough or experienced enough to answer most of their questions, and resist the temptation to do the things you used to do together. Try to just be a good witness to them and whenever you are invited to join them in something that is wrong or a source of temptation to you, just say: "no thanks" and go on your way.

Ask the Lord for His protection and to lead you in the straight and narrow path. As you walk with Him, He'll answer your prayers and show you what to do and what not to do, where to go and where not to go. Make a commitment to pray and read your Bible every day and persevere in it *(Ephesians 6:18)*.

9. Deliver Us From The Evil One

The devil is real, and he is busy in this world doing all kinds of ungodly deeds by using those that are under his power. He is called the prince of this world *(John 12:31)*. The Bible says that the devil has blinded the eyes of the unbelievers that the light of the gospel does not shine on them and be saved *(2 Corinthians 4:3-4)*.

Ask the Lord to protect you from the attacks of the devil and deliver you from his traps. God has assigned an angel to each one of his children to protect and guide them throughout their pilgrimage in this life. Usually other angels are dispatched to help those that are in more intense battlefields in times of danger.

10. For Yours Is The Kingdom, The Power And The Glory Forever And Ever Amen.

Here is where you close your prayer with worship and exaltation of God. You begin prayer with worship, and you end your prayer with worship. Thank Him every day for saving you and giving you the precious Holy Spirit. Remember that we were created to worship God. He loves you to worship Him in spirit and in truth *(John 4:22-24)*.

6

BEING A GOOD STEWARD

In the Word of God, we are instructed to be good stewards *(I Peter 4:10)*. Webster's Dictionary defines a steward as one to whose care is committed the management of a household. One who acts as a supervisor of finances or property for another. One of your duties as a new believer is to support the church with your talents, finances and prayers.

Jesus spoke of a steward who was responsible for what was entrusted to him. To this steward, his master said, *"...Give an account of your stewardship..." (Luke 16:2)*. We are responsible to be a good and faithful steward of basically three things: (1) *our time* (2) *our talents* and (3) *our treasure*. We are not our own *(I Cor. 6:19)*, and each of us shall give an account of himself to God *(Romans 14:12)*.

A. Our Time

As good stewards of God, we are responsible for our time. The most precious commodity that each one of us has is time. Time must not be squandered. Each one of us has been given 24 hours a day. Our success or failure in life depends on how we use our time. We are told by the Apostle Paul to, *"redeem the time..." (Eph.5:15-16)*. This involves knowing what we want to do and how we are going to do it.

1. Goals and Priorities

Managing your time requires self-discipline. This means that you need to have both short-term and long-term goals. If you don't know where you are going, any road will get you there. The faster you travel, the sooner you will get nowhere. When you aim at nothing, you will hit the target. If you don't know where you are going, you will waste valuable time wandering about meaninglessly, and will result in a wasted life. Take time to pray about your objectives in life.

2. Schedules

Time can be abused, wasted, and slept away; or it may be redeemed, conserved, and used wisely for self-improvement, spiritual growth, and the service of others. When you organize your life by a schedule, it sets you free from worry, guilt and the frustration of not doing the important things you need to do daily. There should be a time for prayer and Bible reading. Learn to plan months ahead. This will help you know what you are going to do and when you are going to do it. It will save you untold confusion and frustration.

3. Activities

The *good* things in life are often the enemies of the *best* things in life. You should arrange your activities to do the *best* things with your time. Some questions you can ask yourself are: *(1) will this count ten years from now? (2) Will this count in eternity? (3) Is this helping me reach my goals?* A very helpful tool I like to use is a "*to do*" list. Every night you should do a list of *"to do"* things for the following day in order of importance. As you pray, you will probably add some things to this list rather than forgetting them. *"To do"* lists can be expanded to long-term goals as well.

B. Our Talents

In Matthew 25:14-30 Jesus gave us a parable illustrating the importance of using our talents. We all have something to offer. A beautiful lesson to learn from this parable is that they were not commended for their exploits but for their obedience and faithfulness in using their talents. The man with one talent maybe buried his talent because he felt inferior to his fellow servants. But he was lazy, and misjudged the Lord by thinking He was a hard man, making unjust demands upon his servants. In God's eyes, success is not measured by how famous or important we are or how much money or material goods we have, but whether we have been obedient in using our talents to fulfill His will in our lives.

We serve the Lord out of love and gratitude, not by force *(Hebrews 12:28)*. Make a list of things you can do and the abilities you possess. Find out about opportunities to serve in the local Church, and make yourself available in these areas in which you feel capable. If you have musical talents, a passion for children, youth or any other gifting, put it to use for the Lord. Expect to be used in small things first. In time, an opportunity will present itself and you will be used.

C. Our Treasure

About half of the parables Jesus talks about in the Bible refer to money. In **Matthew 6:21** Jesus talks about our treasures. How people handle money is a pretty good indication of their relationship with God. It has been said that when Jesus saves a man, He saves his pocketbook too. If Jesus is Lord of all, then He is Master of the purse as well. Whenever you give money, give it as unto the Lord, not as though you are giving it to a man. Let's look at some reasons why we should give of our finances to God

1. Because We Love Him

This should be the only reason we need to give to the Lord of the finances that He has blessed us with. God loved us so much that He gave *(John 3:16)*.

2. To Reach the Lost

Our giving helps to reach precious souls with the gospel of Jesus Christ. Salvation is free, but to take the message of salvation to others costs money. The ministers are only able to do their work full time if we support them with our finances *(Romans 10:13-15)*.

God has ordained that His ministers be supported by His people *(Matthew 10:10, I Cor. 9:7-14)*. *Hebrews 7:4-10* declares that, *"here men receive tithes..."* In the book of *Galatians 6:6*, Paul explains that the teachers of divine things should receive ministerial support from those being instructed. We must give according to our blessing and God will bless us according to our giving.

3. Because We Love Our Church Family

We give because we love our church family and want to do our part as responsible members to support it. Remember it takes money to pay the rent, utilities, advertising, maintenance etc. to keep the House of the Lord looking nice so God's people can enjoy it.

4. Because It Is Commanded By God

Anytime someone starts talking about money and tithes, people get defensive. However, this is a divine principle that God established in His kingdom to bless His people. You reap whatever you sow. So if you sow money into good soil *(good ministry, or a good cause)*, you will reap abundantly. The Lord Jesus commanded us to give, and said it would result in blessings for us, in proportion to what we give *(Luke 6:38)*. We are to give our tithe *(10% of income)* and offerings *(any money we give besides the tithe)* to the Lord *(Malachi 3:8-10)*. We should give it cheerfully, not out of necessity *(2 Corinthians 8:12, 9:7)*.

D. Our Family

The Word of God has a lot to say about the home and the relationship among family members. The way you handle your family relationships will affect your walk with God. The enemy will seek to bring strife and confusion into the home of a Christian family. Most problems in marriage relationships are of a spiritual nature, and therefore can only be fixed using spiritual principles. You cannot fix these problems using psychology or worldly remedies. Christ must be included in the equation.

The word of God has clear and powerful teaching to help build solid spiritual lives and homes. God has laid clear-cut lines of authority and responsibility in the family. It is vital to recognize this structure of Divine Order to achieve well being and happiness in the family life.

1. Divine Order for the Family

There is a divine order of authority, which is spoken of in the Bible. Jesus spoke on the subject of authority many times, so did the apostle Paul in several of his epistles. The principles of Divine Order are outlined below and should be studied carefully. Jesus Christ is the head of the husband, and Lord of the family *(I Corinthians 11:3).* The husband lives under the authority of Christ and is responsible to Christ for the leadership and care of the family. He needs to love and honor his wife, protect her and provide for her needs.

The wife lives under the authority of her husband and needs to submit, respect and reverence him *(Ephesians 5:24-33).* The children live under the authority of both parents and are commanded to honor and obey them in everything *(Colossians 3:20).* Any change from this will only bring forth a dysfunctional family for which there is no cure-except a return to God's original order.

2. Submission

Submission is one of the most beautiful and powerful concepts in the New Testament. To be submissive means to yield humble and intelligent obedience to an ordained power of authority. God did not have a grudge against women when He gave this commandment. He established it for the protection of women and the harmony of the home. God never forces anyone to submit, but He honors only those who choose freely this role.

3. Respect and Reverence

The fullest definition of this word can be found in the Amplified New Testament: "Let the wife see that she respects and reverences her husband-that she notices him, regards him, honors him, prefers him, venerates and esteems him; and that she defers to him, praises him, and loves and admires him exceedingly."

4. Love and Honor

The husband is explicitly commanded to love and honor his wife. Please note in Ephesians 5 that the husband is told three times to love his wife. Although the scriptures place great emphasis on the submission of the wife, they also put equally strong emphasis on the fact that the husband must love his wife. There will be times when the husband feels anything but affection for her. However, love is not primarily a feeling, but a choice for the other's highest good. The husband must get his emotions under control and do what is right. He must learn to forgive and show Christ-likeness love. Without it, his prayers will be hindered and his marriage doomed to failure.

7

SHARING THE GOSPEL

One of your responsibilities after you are born again is to evangelize other people by sharing your testimony *(Mark 16:15-16)*. Tell others what God has done for you. There are many sad and lonely people, living empty lives out there that desperately need the experience you have with God. It is the responsibility of every believer to share the gospel with his family, friends and neighbors who do not know the Lord and are headed for eternity without Christ. The Lord gave us supernatural power to be His witnesses when we received the Holy Spirit *(Acts 1:8)*. He told us to go and promised to be with us always *(Luke 15:4-10)*.

We are sent forth as sheep in the midst of wolves. Jesus told us to be wise as serpents and gentle as doves *(Matthew 10:16)*. The gospel must be preached boldly, with love and a great deal of wisdom. The wisest man that ever lived said: "He that wins souls is wise *(Proverbs 11:30)*. Soul winning is a spiritual business. It is our duty to prepare ourselves with the word of God and be ready to share it with someone else *(I Peter 3:15)*. Some people think that because they do not know much about the Bible, they are not able to share the gospel effectively with anyone. But a person with an argument is no match for a person with an experience. You have had a real, personal experience with God, and that is something that no one can deny. What can they say? It happened to you! You are living proof of the power of the gospel of Jesus Christ to change a life *(Romans 1:16)*. The thought will come to them, *"if it happened to them, it can happen to me as well."*

A. How To Be A Witness

Sharing your testimony is the most effective and exciting way of winning souls. If you walk upright before God and men, your words are going to have authority. You can only be an effective soul winner when your words line up with your lifestyle. If you live right and don't tell anyone about it, how will they know unless they are told? On the other hand, if you say you are a Christian but walk in the flesh, and do not have the fruit of the Spirit, it brings reproach to the Lord *(Galatians 5:19-23)*.

We should not be ashamed of the gospel or be a shame to the gospel. If you are witnessing to someone and you are committing adultery or having sex with someone outside of marriage, puffing cigarette smoke in his or her face, have a beer can in your hand and are reeking with body odor, do you think you will be a credible witness? When the Lord saves someone, He also wants to set him free from these different strongholds *(Isaiah 61:1-1; John 8:36)*. Now let's take a look at some pointers on witnessing.

1. Do Not Argue Or Judge

Keep in mind that we are called to be witnesses, not lawyers who argue, judges who judge people, or defendants who defend the gospel. *You only need to speak the things you have seen and heard (Acts 4:20).* People get defensive when you criticize their doctrines or religious beliefs. Remember they think they are right, and you will never convince them that they are wrong by winning the argument with them. Just tell them that there is a real personal experience with a loving God available to them.

Some of them may be holding on to religious beliefs passed down to them by people they dearly loved. When you criticize their beliefs, in their minds you are criticizing their loved ones. You may win the argument, but you will not win them to the Lord. Try to make them understand that there is more for them than the religious experience they may already have.

2. Use the Before and After Technique

This is the same formula advertising companies use when they want to sell you a product. They don't waste their time trying to explain to you the formulas they used in the product; they just use before and after pictures to convince you. Because most people only seek God when they are in a desperate situation, in your own words describe briefly how you were before the Lord found you, and what led you to seek Him.

For example: *"I had no desire to live anymore"*, *"I had an addiction"*, or *"I felt rejected, lonely and empty deep inside"* and so on. Then share with them in detail what happened to you after you were born again. Be specific, for example: *"I don't feel empty or rejected anymore, now I have joy"*, *"I don't curse anymore, and I feel incredible peace now"* *"I was bound by addiction, but now I am free"* and so on.

This is what the blind man in the 9th chapter of John did when interrogated by the Jewish court on how Jesus had miraculously given him his sight. He responded to all their difficult theological questions with a simple answer based on his own personal experience. When the Pharisees accused Jesus of being a sinner, he simply replied, *"...whether he is a sinner or not I don't know: one thing I do know, that I was blind and now I see."*

The apostle Paul used this same technique when he was brought before kings and religious leaders to answer for his faith. Of all people, Paul could have tried to influence them with his logic and great knowledge of the scriptures. But instead, he used the most powerful weapon in defense of the gospel: *his personal testimony.* He told them of his life before he knew the Lord Jesus, how he was converted, and what he was like afterwards.

B. How to Lead Others to Jesus

Leading a soul to the feet of the cross of Jesus is one of most important and beautiful moments in the life of a Christian. A soul is worth more than all the gold in the whole world. When we leave this world, we will not be able to take anything with us. Only the souls we have won to the Lord and that which is done for Christ will remain. Let's take a look at what you need to do, depending on the situation.

1. When People Are Hungry And Receptive

There will be times when you share your testimony, that you may find someone who is hungry and receptive to know more about God. A person does not necessarily have to be in a church altar to be saved. They can be on the job, street, restaurant, in a store, anywhere! When this happens, you need to know how to lead them to salvation by using a few scriptures.

When the opportunity presents itself, say to the person, *"would you mind if I share some scriptures with you?"* Share with them the following scriptures quoting it to them one by one or use a small pocket New Testament: *(a) Romans 3:23 (2) Romans 6:23 (3) Romans 5:8 and finally (4) Acts 2:36-38.* After you share these scriptures with them, you may ask them, *"Do you believe Jesus Christ died for you?"* If they say yes, then say, "Do you want to receive Jesus as your Lord and Savior right now?" If they say yes, ask them to repent of their sins, and pray with them. Repentance is a very important step to salvation *(Luke 13:5, Acts 17:30, Acts 2:38).*

The reason repentance is so important is because it is the first and most essential step that every soul must take. Without repentance, no one can be born again and receive God's Spirit. Without repentance, baptism in water is meaningless. We need to lead the souls to the cross first and then to church. Unrepentant souls are usually hesitant about going to church. However, when someone repents, they are more responsive, usually want to go to church and hear more about God. We can lead a soul to Jesus Christ anytime and anyplace.

2. When People Are Hard And Unreceptive

If a person does not respond to anything that we have shared with you so far, maybe it is because they believe that they are good, and don't need to be saved. Many people think that doing good things saves them. Others do not believe in Jesus at all. These need to be persuaded that they are sinners, and without Jesus they are going to hell *(Romans 3:23).*

This is where the law of God plays a very significant role. This is the purpose of the law, to make people feel guilty. Ask them the following questions: *(1) have you ever lied?* Most honest people will answer *yes.* Then you ask them the second question: *(2) what does that make you?* If they are honest, they will say, *a liar.* Then ask them the third question: *(3) do you know that the Bible says that liars will go to hell?*

Repeat this process of asking the person three questions using other commandments like: *Stealing, and adultery.* If the person becomes receptive, then ask them if they believe Jesus Christ died for them? If they say yes, take through the process in the previous section.

If they say no, do not feel rejected, simply say, "I understand your feelings and respect your decision. If you

45

ever decide to give your life to Jesus remember He loves you and will be waiting for you with His arms wide open." This will release the pressure and leaves the door open for the future. Sometimes you may not be the one to reap the fruit of the seed you planted. However, you will have had a part in the salvation of such a one when they make their decision for Christ in the future and are saved.

Whenever you talk about God and try to win others to the Lord, you will pay a price. Expect to be criticized, persecuted, and rejected even by your own family. His own family called Jesus crazy, and others called Him a glutton and a winebibber. He told us to expect the same. You must be willing to be rejected and criticized for His sake *(Mathew 10:37-39, 22:37)*.

C. Baptism Of Water And Spirit

Once the person has repented, explain this is only the first step, and that there is more for them. Share with the person the importance of being baptized in water and receiving the Holy Spirit baptism. Once again, tell them your personal testimony, and how wonderful it is to have the Spirit of the Lord living within you, and being able to talk to Him in a heavenly tongue.

For more information on water baptism and the baptism of the Holy Spirit, see chapters two and three in this book.

8

WORSHIPPING IN SPIRIT & IN TRUTH

All over the world, there is a word that is used to express praise to God, and is the same is every language. It is the word HALLELUJAH, which literally means, "Praise the Lord." Other phrases such as, "Glory to God," and "Praise the Lord," is also common among born again believers. This is because the Bible is filled with exhortations to praise God for all His wondrous works. Praise is natural for all that know God. When a person experiences salvation, sees God for who He really is and what He has done and can do, praise comes forth spontaneously. Worship reverences God for who He is!

A. Worship

The first mention of the word, worship, in the Bible is found in *Genesis 22:5*. God asked Abraham to offer his only son, and he was obedient to the voice of the Lord. He did not know what the final result would be, but he had complete confidence in God. He honored and reverenced God and obeyed His word. This is true worship. Thousands of years later, Jesus approached the woman in Samaria and explained to her the meaning of true worship *(John 4:23-24)*. Because God is a spiritual being, He must be worshipped in reality and sincerity-in a spiritual way.

In both Hebrew and Greek, the word worship means to fall or bow down before God in homage. This can be taken figuratively or literally, but it speaks of one's attitude more than anything else does. If we bowed down before Him, but did not surrender our will, it would not

47

mean a thing. Worship does not require a special audience or place. It is not a respector of nationalities, languages or cultures. Neither is it dependent upon wealth, age or education. The only thing that matters is the sincerity of the individual offering it, because worship is the way we adore and reverence our God.

When we first came to God, the first thing that had to change was our attitude. What we thought of God changed, and we began to recognize Him for what He has always been. We see Him as the angelic hosts see Him: King of kings and Lord of lords. Worship adores and honors God for all that He is to us. All that He is to us depends upon our attitudes. Our attitudes are how we really think. Let's take a look at three attitudes that our worship depends on.

1. Our Attitude Toward God

When we worship, there must be an object of worship. The object of our worship is God, and *Deuteronomy 6:5* tells us to worship or love Him with all of our heart, soul and might. The Bible stated clearly that we should not worship anything but God *(Leviticus 26:1)*. The first chapter of *Romans* explains the danger of half-hearted or insincere worship. When people worship and serve the creature rather than the Creator, their hearts become fearfully darkened and their lives become exceedingly corrupt.

2. Our Attitude Toward Men

Because man is made in the image of God, it is impossible to worship God and mistreat or ignore our fellowman and brethren in Christ *(Matthew 25:40)*. Our attitude toward God is reflected by our attitude toward our brethren *(John 13:35, I John 4:20-21)*. Our true love (worship) toward God demands that we have a right

48

attitude toward our brethren. If there is conflict between you and your brother, you have to resolve it before you worship God *(Matthew 5:23-34)*.

3. Our Attitude Toward Circumstances

Since we have discovered that worship begins with a correct attitude, we will be able to worship God continually. We can worship at home, on the job, at school, in the market…everywhere! We should worship God when things are going wrong as well as when things are going good, and in times of sorrow as well as in times of rejoicing. As soon as Job learned he had lost most of his possessions, and all his children, the Bible says he fell down upon the ground, and worshipped God and said, "The Lord giveth, and the Lord taketh away; blessed be the name of the Lord."

B. Forms Of Praise

When Christians get together; spontaneous expressions of praise and worship take place. Some of the most important times in your life will be when you are worshipping God with all your heart together with His people. This is because God manifests Himself as we praise Him *(Psalms 22:3)*. Pentecostal and Charismatic believers are known for their lively, exuberant worship. Here are some of these forms of praise:

1. Giving Testimonies

Giving a testimony of something God has done for you is something that should flow naturally out of every believer *(Luke 12:8, Psalms 66:16)*. You should never hold back from giving glory to God through your personal testimony. It will bless those that hear it.

2. Worshiping God with Uplifted Hands

One of the most beautiful expressions of worship is when a Christian sincerely lifts his/her hands to offer God a sacrifice of praise. It is an act of surrender, just like a doggie lies with his paws up, as an act of surrender to his master *(Psalms 134:2, I Tim. 2:8)*.

3. Pray Out Aloud

We should pray privately in our secret closet, but we should also pray out loud with other believers *(Psalms 116:17, Acts 4:24)*.

4. Worship with a loud noise & dance

Worshipping God with a loud noise and dance is one of the oldest forms of worship. Some people prefer not to be so exuberant in their demonstration of love and worship to God and that is fine, as long as they don't become critical of those who do *(Psalms 98:4, 149:3, 150:4)*.

5. Applause

This is another one of the oldest forms of praise found not only in the Bible, but also in cultures all over the world *(Psalms 47:1).* Read the book of Psalms for the greatest collection of praises ever.

9

SPIRITUAL WARFARE

When you gave your heart to Jesus Christ, you inadvertently were enlisted in His army and consequently entered into spiritual conflict with the forces of the enemy of God. This is a fight to the end, in which we must learn how to persevere and win. In the Bible we are told to fight the good fight of faith *(I Timothy 6:12).*

Whether you realize it or not, you have already been engaged in some of the battles. It is not a physical warfare you are fighting. The battle and the weapons we use in the battle are spiritual, and the battlefield is our mind. Here is where victories are won and defeats are suffered. God's promise is that He will keep our hearts and minds through Jesus Christ *(Philippians 4:7).*

However, in order for us to be victorious, we must know our enemy, his tactics and his weapons. In addition, we must learn how to put on the whole armor the Lord provided us with, and learn how to use it if we are going to be victorious in the daily battles in our lives *(I Corinthians 15:57; Ephesians 6:10-18).*

A. Our Enemies

Every Christian has three enemies that oppose and resist him every day of his life in his pilgrimage on this earth. Two of them are outward, and one is inward. They are known as the world, the devil and the flesh. If you are going to be successful as a Christian, you must know each one of them, and learn how to overcome them. Let's take a look at each one of them.

1. The World

The Bible says that the whole world is under the control of the evil one *(I John 5:19)*. We are told not to love the world nor the things that are in the world *(I John 2:15-16)*. The world will never love us or recognize us because it never loved Jesus *(I John 3:1).*

Those that are of the world are loved by the world and the world hears them because they speak the same language of the world. However, we are of God *(I John 4:5). James 4:4* gives us a sober warning: "Know you not that the friendship of the world is enmity with God? Whosoever therefore will be a friend of the world is the enemy of God."

2. The Devil

Since you became a child of God, the devil is exceedingly angry at you, and will use all of his wiles to lure you back to him. If you are foolish enough to listen to him, he will cause you untold misery, suffering, and will try to destroy your home, family, health, finances and if he can, your soul. "Be sober, be vigilant; because your adversary the devil, as a roaring lion prowls about, seeking whom he may devour." *(I Pet. 5:8).*

3. The Flesh

The only one of the three enemies that is within us is what the Bible calls the flesh. We obtained this carnal, fleshly, sinful nature from our parents, who got it from their parents, and so forth all the way back to our first parents Adam and Eve, who received this evil nature from the devil when they first sinned in the Garden of Eden.

This sinful nature was passed on to each succeeding generation until we have it today. This is the "flesh", our inward enemy. Peter tells us in his first epistle to abstain from fleshly lusts which war against the soul *(I Pet. 2:11)*. Paul tells us in **Romans 8:8** and **Galatians 5:17** that they that are in the flesh can't please God.

B. The Enemy's Weapon

One of Satan's major weapons is temptation *(Mathew 4:3).* He often uses worldly attractions to tempt us, just like he did with Jesus. He plants thoughts and ideas in your mind like a computer virus, and makes you think it came from you, when in fact it came from him. Why is it Jesus resisted the temptation of the devil and the world but so often Christians do not? We all have the power to resist. Jesus has given us all the spiritual resources necessary to resist but many times we do not recognize temptation when it comes to us, and lack the willpower to resist it and say no.

The reason we fail when confronted with temptations is because the carnal nature in us responds to the temptation and wants to sin *(James 1:15).* The response of the flesh to temptation is called lust, and comes in various forms. It may come as a desire to do something sinful or worldly. It may manifest as a doubt, as an urge to be a show off or be rebellious against those in authority over you. It may come in a thousand shapes or forms, but it is always from the devil and it is the devil's big weapon in spiritual warfare *(I Corinthians 10:13; I John 1:9, 4:4).*

C. The Armor Of God

The Bible compares us to soldiers *(2 Timothy 2:4).* There is a reason why the apostle Paul used the military armor worn by the Roman soldiers of his day to explain the Christian's spiritual armor. Paul says that these weapons are mighty *(I Corinthians 10:4).* Paul tells us to put on the whole armor of God and do battle in the form of prayer *(Ephesians 6:18)*. There are five pieces of armor and two weapons given to us *(Ephesians 6:13-18)*. The five pieces of armor are to protect ourselves against the enemy. The two weapons given to us are to defend ourselves as well as to attack.

1. The Breastplate Of Righteousness

Just like the breastplate used by the roman soldiers protected their vital organs from being injured, the breastplate of righteousness covers our heart & inward parts. We will never be able to defend ourselves when the devil accuses us of not being righteous, if we don't appropriate the righteousness of Jesus Christ *(Romans 3:20-28; 4:1-22; 10:3-10; 2 Corinthians 5:21; Galatians 4:24)*. When we confess with our mouths that we have been made righteous by the blood of the Lamb, the enemy can't accuse you anymore of not been righteous enough.

2. The Belt Of Truth

In the Roman soldier's uniform, it was the belt that held the sword in place. If the belt was not fastened correctly, the soldier was not able to use the sword effectively. You must have the belt of Truth on correctly if you are going to wield the sword of the Spirit effectively. When we were born again, we received the Spirit of Truth *(John 15:26)*.

The Holy Spirit will lead you into all truth if you ask Him. He is best qualified to interpret scriptures. Only when we use the Spirit of Truth are we able to use the Bible correctly. There are many who twist the scriptures to fit their own particular doctrine, personal belief or agenda to their own destruction. We must align our beliefs and doctrines to the Word of God, not the other way around.

3. The Shoes of The Gospel of Peace

The Roman soldiers were equipped with special kind of boots whose soles were so tough that it protected them against rocks, nails and the sort. In the heat of battle, if a soldier injures his feet or looses his footing, he may be severely wounded or even killed. Likewise, we have received the peace of God to protect us in this world *(John 14:27, 16:33).* The sons of God are called to be peacemakers and live in peace with each other *(Mathew 5:9; Mark 9:50).* Our feet should always go in the way of peace *(Luke 1:79, 2:14, 10:5).*

After the resurrection, every time Jesus met his disciples He pronounced peace upon them *(John20:19-26).* The early church walked in peace and the comfort of the Holy Spirit *(Acts 9:31).* The gospel we preach is a gospel of peace *(Ephesians 6:15).* Demons love arguments and strife because it takes away peace and puts us in a dangerous position. We should always try to control our actions and conversation to reflect the peace of God.

4. The Shield Of Faith

The shield the Roman soldiers used was so big that it almost covered all of their body. It was made of a special kind of material that put out all the fiery arrows of the enemy when they hit the shield. Remember to use your faith to protect yourself from evil attacks. Faith is like a muscle, it grows stronger the more you use it. You need to exercise your faith daily. You can find out what the definition of faith is by reading *Hebrews 11*.

5. The Helmet Of Salvation

The helmet was one of the most important part of the equipment used by the Roman soldier. It protected his head from severe injury and death. A person can withstand a blow to any part of the body and keep going, but a blow to the head can disable him or kill him.

The mind is where the fiercest and most important battles are going to be fought in your life as a Christian *(2 Corinthians 10:3-5)*. It is the seat of your soul, which is your emotions and personality. A man becomes what he thinks about *(Proverbs 23:7)*. When you were born again, your spirit was renewed, but not your mind. You have to renew your mind by reading of the Word of God daily *(Romans 12:2)*. Study the Bible and learn what the Word of God says about you.

6.   The Sword Of The Spirit

The Roman sword was a formidable weapon. It was the strongest sword of its day. The Word of God is the sword of the Spirit. This is one of the offensive weapons, but it can be a powerful defensive weapon as well *(Hebrews 4:12)*.

Whenever the devil tempted the Lord, He defended Himself with the Word of God *(Luke 4:1-14)*. If the Lord used the Word of God against the devil, we should follow His example. That is why the Word of God is called the sword of the Spirit. It can cut through any argument, deceit, lie or deception the devil may throw at you.

7.   Prayer And Supplications

This is the second weapon the Lord has given us, and it is most powerful when combined with the Word of God. You should never underestimate the power of prayer in the life of a Christian. Always remember this: *much prayer, much power; little prayer, little power*. The enemy is terrified of the weakest saint when they get down on their knees to pray.

10

DISCOVERING YOUR SPIRITUAL GIFTS AND MINISTRY

One of the biggest tragedies in the Church today is the lack of participation from ninety percent of the body in the Kingdom of God. Most believers have no idea what their gifts are, and what ministry they have been given to do by the Lord on this earth. As I travel throughout the country, when I ask the believers in different churches to raise their hands if they know what their particular gifts and ministries are, less than ten percent raise their hands. Without a proper emphasis on the place of the Holy Spirit in the life of the believer and the church, there will be no real spiritual life and power in the church to minister to the needs of people.

The Lord wants His church to become a functional body, manifesting their God given talents and abilities to fulfill their mission in this world. In order to achieve this, the Church has to be taught that they were not saved to be mere spectators, but to be an active part in what God is doing on the earth today. If we are going to do this, we have to come to the understanding that every part of the body is useful, different, and performs a different function one from another. Many believers never attempt to do anything because they think they have to do it like somebody else.

God is a very creative and diverse being and nature reflects this truth. Everybody is not supposed to be the same, and do things the same way. We need the whole body in order to fulfill the great commission in this last day. This lesson deals with highly important phases of the operation of the Holy Spirit in the believer's life, in the church and in the whole sphere of the church body.

A. You Have a Spiritual Gift

Very few believers today are exercising their gifts that they received from their heavenly Father in their lives. This stems from either the fact that they ignore that they have at least one spiritual gift from God, or because they seem to think spiritual gifts can only operate through those who are exceptionally spiritual, and thus, worthy of the gift. But this is an erroneous belief. The church at Corinth is proof that the possession of gifts is not to be equated with maturity or perfection in the life of the believer *(1 Corinthians 3:1-4, 5:1-13)*. Because you are a member of God's family, you have at least one gift. This gift gives you a place and function in the body.

There is no one member in your physical body without a specific function it performs. This is important because many people don't believe they have a spiritual gift and this prevents them from ever being able to use the gift they were given *(1 Corinthians 12:7-27)*. Peter also confirms the fact that there is no one who has not received a gift to minister to someone else. All are to be stewards of the grace of God. That means that they are to properly handle the gifts given to them by God *(I Peter 4:10-11)*.

B. Gifts Versus Fruit

A gift says nothing about the character of the believer, it only reveals the character of the giver. A gift is just that, and it is not deserved or earned, or it would not be a gift. Since many believers think that the gifts of the Spirit can only operate in the life of one who is spiritually mature, of sterling character, and perfect in every way, they reject any operation of a gift through anyone who does not measure up to these qualifications. Then, when in their view, the gifts operate through a person, they tend to idolize that individual as one who is far advanced spiritually, and he may be, but then again, this is the difference between gifts and fruit.

The gifts of the Spirit are given freely, regardless of spiritual maturity. There is no evidence that the person operating them has advanced spiritually. The fruit of the spirit *(Galatians 5:22-23)* however, gives evidence of spiritual maturity. It tells us something about the person's character and their spiritual condition.

C. You Have A Ministry

The word *minister* in the Bible means *servant*. Every believer is not called to the five-fold ministry, which are apostle, prophet, evangelist, pastor and teacher. But every believer is called to minister to others according to the gifts and talents they received from God *(Ephesians 4:11-14)*. In *Romans 12:3-8,* Paul says that every member of the body of Jesus Christ has a motivational gift, which serves as his primary vehicle for ministry.

Everyone has at least one spiritual gift, which compliments or helps to do that motivational gift or ministry. Therefore, the ministry or motivational gift you have received from the Lord, according to *Romans 12:3-8* will often be expressed through and/or assisted by the spiritual gift. The spiritual gift you have will, in all probabilities, serve to administer that motivational gift (ministry), and will help you identify it and activate it in your own life.

D. How You Can Identify Your Spiritual Gift

There are three major keys to identifying the spiritual gift God has given you. They are *desire, ability and confirmation (Ephesians 2:10, Phillipians 2:13 and I Timothy 1:6)*. First, we should notice that God puts or gives desires in us to will. What gifts are you most interested in? God placed the desire for these gifts in you.

In other words, we are incapable of doing any good thing *(Romans 3:12)*. Since it is a good thing to desire spiritual things, we can be sure that this desire is not of ourselves; it is of God. He put that desire in us.

Secondly, God works in us to give us the ability to do that which He gives us the desire and will to do. God will never give us the desire to do something that He will not give us the ability to do. Therefore, if you have a specific desire related to spiritual gifts, you can be sure that *God put that desire in you*. If He has given you the desire for a certain gift, He will surely give you the ability to minister this gift or gifts. There is nothing wrong about desiring spiritual gifts *(1 Corinthians 12:31, 14:1)*.

The third thing is confirmation of the particular gift God has given you. This means that if God has truly given you a spiritual gift or gifts, you will not be the only one who knows it. Others who recognize that the operation of the gifts through you is genuine will confirm it. Whichever ministry or gift you have received from God, you will identify it by being good at it, and enjoy doing it. Beware of wrong desires based on pride or greed. God will not reward selfish desires *(James 4:3)*. However, if your desires are pure and you want to be used of God to help hurting people, even if no fame or wealth comes to you as a result of it, God will use you in the gifts of the Holy Spirit to minister to the hurting and bless you.

Be patient and understand that your gift will make a way for you eventually. In the next chapter, we will look at some of the ways that you will know when the time comes for you to be used of God. If God truly called you to the five-fold ministry, it will not go away. It is yours and nobody can take it away from you. No one else can cash it in because God gave it to you. It will take time for the Lord to process you so He can use you the way He wants to. Be patient, and enjoy every phase of you walk with God. Get to know Him intimately and become His very best friend.

11

KNOWING GOD'S WILL

One of the most difficult things for people to understand is that God does not think like we think. People tend to measure God by their own temperaments and capabilities. But His ways are beyond our ways *(Romans 11:33)*. The natural mind can't comprehend that which is of the spirit. So if we are going to understand God's will, we must take a look at His nature and His purposes as found in the Bible.

A. His Nature

Jesus came to earth to reveal to us the heart of the Father. When we read about Jesus in the gospels, we see how He treats the children; speaks gently to the poor; weeps with friends who are suffering and in pain; respond to critics with wisdom, righteousness and authority, and He wept for Jerusalem. As you read the Bible, you will find out that God is:

1. Rational

God has incredible common sense. I have found out that everything the Lord does has common sense at its deepest level of reasoning. God does not loose His head in a crisis situation. He does not make poor judgments. His nerves don't go to pieces under pressure. Jesus never retaliated when He was falsely accused or wronged in any way. He always kept His cool.

2. Constant

God never changes *(Malachi 3:6)*. He is never depressed, confused or perplexed. He knows the end from the beginning *(Isaiah 46:10)*. He is committed to His Word. Whatever God said, He will bring it to pass. Anytime He says something, He stands by His word.

3. Holy

God's character is holy *(Isaiah 6:3)*. Everything He does is compatible with His character. He is incapable of doing anything sinful, wrong or unjust. He is completely righteous and just in all His decisions and dealings.

4. Love

God is love. He loves His people with an amazing kind of love. Agape love, the kind of love that loves even the unlovable, without expecting back anything. While we were yet sinners, Christ died for us *(Romans 5:8)*. That is love.

5. Merciful

One of the most distinctive attributes of God is that He is merciful. God is quick to forgive, and slow to anger, rich in mercy and grace *(Exodus 34:6; Ephesians 2:4-7; Hebrews 8:12)*.

B. His Purposes

God has a purpose. He is not willing that any should perish, but that all men should be saved *(II Peter 3:9)*. The salvation of people is very dear to the Heart of the Lord. God always uses men to perform His will, and achieve His purposes *(Luke 4:18-19).* Let's take a look at some of the things that is God's will and desire to do:

1. To Save All Men

God wants to save the lost, without regard of race, nationality, sex or age *(Romans 10:13-15).* He does genuinely love and is interested in the welfare of all human beings. This in itself is a great mystery.

2. To Heal the Sick and Brokenhearted

God wants His children to be healed and have healthy lives. It is not God's will for people to be sick and oppressed. By His stripes we are healed *(Isaiah 61:1-3; I Peter 2:24).*

3. To Deliver

Jesus came to save humanity in every way we could be saved: body, soul and spirit *(Isaiah 61).* All Christians believe God wants to save them from their sins. But not all believe that He genuinely wants to heal and deliver them from sickness, disease, strongholds and bondages that bind them. Jesus came to set the captives free *(Luke 7:21, 8:2; Acts 10:38,19:12).*

4. To Reconcile

Jesus came to reconcile men back to God. God's will is that we all be reconciled to Him, and then that we should all be reconciled and love one another. He wants unity and peace to come to His Body, so that the world may believe *(John 17:9-26; 2 Corinthians 5:19).*

C. His Will for You

The key to discovering the will of God is the word *available*. Paul told the early Christians to present their bodies a living sacrifice, holy, acceptable unto God *(Romans 12:1)*. He knows better than anybody else the gifts, talents and abilities He has placed within you. Those gifts were placed there to help you fulfill your calling on this earth *(Ephesians 3:10)*. The first thing to do when making any decision is to be sure you do everything in harmony with three things.

These are like three traffic lights of God's will that must all be green before you proceed. When one of the three is red, stop there and don't go any further. If it is green, go to the next light of God's will. A yellow light means wait. Finally when the third light of God's will is green, you can proceed at the proper speed. You now have the mind and timing of the Lord, so finalize the decision by taking immediate action.

1. The Word Of God

Most Christians are diligent to obey God's Word. If a dream, prophetic word, or a message from someone does not line up with the word of God, that is a red light to stop and not do it. The word of God is the plumb line to which everything must line up to. No matter how good something sounds, if it goes against the word of God don't do it. God's Word is general and may not apply to your situation. That's when you need to know...

2. The Specific Will Of God

To find out the specific will of God for your life you must be willing to wait on Him. God has ordained works for you to walk in them from the foundation of the world.

You just need to discover it. Many Christians seek God's Will on a matter, but have problems with…

3. The Ways Of God

Most Christians are not faithful to wait until God's ways has been made clear. The ways of God includes His timing, methods, and the means to do it. Isaiah says His thoughts are not our thoughts, and His ways are not our ways *(Isaiah 55:7-9)*.

God has a general will for everyone, but He also has a specific will for each person. In the Bible, the Lord offers general directions for all believers, but it contains no specific directions for individuals. However, He does have a specific will for each person on this earth. All true rhemas, dreams, visions and words from God will be in harmony with His overall purposes for your life.

Just as the function of the eyes is not the same as that of the ears or any other part of the body, Christ's specific instructions for each member in the body is not the same. These instructions are personal, and vary from individual to individual. God deals with each person different, but He uses a process of breaking that takes time, in order to prepare his servants for use in His kingdom. It is during this process that He usually reveals His perfect will to us.

D. God's Ways for Revealing His Perfect Will

God's greatest delight is for His children to desire to do His will. He has no desire nor will He ever pressure His children to do His will. If we delight ourselves in the Lord and in doing His will, He will give us the desires of our hearts *(Psalms 37:4)*. Following are some methods to discover God's perfect will for our lives:

1. Rhema and Scripture Illumination

A rhema is an inspired word birthed within your own spirit. It is a whisper, like the still, small voice that spoke to Elijah in the cave. It is a divinely inspired impression upon our souls, a flash of thought or creative idea from God. It is conceived in our spirits, but birthed into your natural understanding by divine illumination. A true rhema has a deep inner assurance and witness of the Spirit. Other times we get a rhema by illumination of a particular scripture. You will have a knowing that this word applies to you.

2. The Prophet and Personal Prophecy

God still uses prophets today to give specific, directive words to the saints about their personal lives. We should always consider carefully any prophetic word given to us. But when a person with a proven ministry gives you a word, and you neither relate to it nor have a witness to it, then you should wait for confirmation. Words, which are not scriptural or are not clearly from God, should be rejected.

Prophecy is heaven's permission to do what you are supposed to do on the earth. Sound always precedes light in the natural; it is the same in the spirit. A prophetic word has the power to fulfill itself. Power is released when you say what God is saying. Therefore, it behooves you to line up your language with what God is doing and speaking into your life.

3. The Gifts Of The Holy Spirit

The Holy Spirit can make known to us the specific will of God through His nine gifts, especially the revelation gifts of the word of knowledge and wisdom. We desperately need these gifts to make wise decisions in our lives, businesses and churches. The gifts of the Holy Spirit are not only for the super spiritual or five-fold ministers, but also for the average Christian to benefit from in their everyday lives.

A choice between right and wrong is not difficult for a dedicated Christian. But in order to make the right choice between two right things, supernatural help is needed. That is why the Lord has given us the gifts of the Spirit. If you need additional teaching on this subject, we have a book available titled: *"Introduction To Signs And Wonders"* that will help you understand the nine gifts of the Spirit and how to use them.

4.   The Fruit of the Holy Spirit

To be led of the Spirit does not mean that we are led only by supernatural manifestations of the Holy Spirit. The fruit of the Spirit is just as vital in determining the mind of Christ as the gifts. The fruit and gifts are like two sides of the same coin, and both sides must be in good shape. To make decisions according to the spiritual peace they bring is being led by the Spirit. To take action because of the joy of the Lord is to be motivated by the Holy Spirit. To move in faith, which is both a gift and a fruit of the Holy Spirit, is moving in the Spirit.

In determining the will of God on a matter look inside your soul and spirit to see how much peace and joy you have about the situation. Do you have faith or doubt, love or fear, joy or anxiety, peace or pressure, meekness or self-will, temperance or impatience? If you have a check in your spirit, then the traffic light of God's will has not turned green.

Do not do anything. Do not make any final decisions until you feel the promptings of the Holy Spirit giving you the green light go ahead. Those gut feelings we often have, God gave them to us to guide us in this life and to help us make the right decisions.

5. Confirmation

One of the best ways for determining the will of God is the requirement of two or three witnesses confirming something as fact. This principle was established by Moses and re-established by Paul in the Church *(Deuteronomy 17:6; 2 Corinthians 13:1).* This can come through a word of knowledge, wisdom, prophecy, a rhema or anything else.

Unity is also a sign of confirmation about an issue or a particular decision. For example a husband and wife when they are in agreement about a decision, it is a good sign of God's will. Unity with other people also applies. That is why the Bible says that in the multitude of counselors there is wisdom *(Proverbs 11:14).*

E. The Way of the Lord

The Word of the Lord comes from heaven to bring direction, order and peace. It is the authorization from Heaven; God's will specifying that a course of action is for you. To fulfill the Way of God, you need above all things patience. Often God's Word and Will are much easier to determine than His Way. This is a process that we must walk out day by day, because the details are rarely ever revealed ahead of time.

The Lord is reluctant to give too many details all at once. So they come one piece at a time, like a real life jigsaw puzzle. Remember God will put you through a learning process before He will use you. He is more interested in your character, and how you respond to different situations and handle certain things, than in you being successful. There are some things the Lord wants to teach you about Him and about yourself. So be very patient, your time in the sunlight will come.

12

BECOMING LIKE JESUS

In this lesson we are going to take a look at some of the principles we need to practice in our lives if we want to become like Jesus. A disciple is one who tries to imitate the one whom he is following. A true disciple will try to talk like Jesus, act like Jesus and think like Jesus. There are some major differences between a believer and a disciple. Jesus commanded us to make disciples of all the nations *(Mathew 28:19-20)*. Let's look at some of the things that characterize a true disciple of Jesus Christ.

A. The Disciple Is Not Above His Master

Everyone who wants to be a disciple of the Lord Jesus Christ must embrace his own cross and follow Him; the path of suffering, faithfulness and consecration that He followed. Jesus spent long hours in communion with the Father, and so must we if are to be like Him.

Prayer to Him was more important than teaching, preaching, hobbies or any pastime. He withdrew to the wilderness to pray *(Luke 5:15)*. Miracles, signs and wonders don't happen by themselves. A life of prayer and consecration is the cause. A disciple will not attain the same results that Jesus did without paying the same price; we are not above the Master *(Matthew 10:24)*.

B. Everyone That is Perfect Shall Be As His Master

We could do the same works Jesus did, because the Lord can't lie *(Luke 6:40, Matthew 5:48)*. However, this is based on conditions and requirements we need to meet.

As a man Jesus was tempted, needed food, rest and sleep. He suffered hunger, thirst, pain, loneliness and weariness. If we are to be His disciples, and manifest the character and power He manifested in His life, we must be like Him in holiness, consecration, meekness and compassion.

We must be like Him in prayer and communion with the Father, faith, fasting and self-denial. We should not make excuses for living a life full of sin and imperfections, but learn to deal with them. If you need deliverance, there is help available for you in the body. But most of the time, it is an issue of flesh and lack of discipline in people's lives.

Sin will drain you of God's presence and power in your life. Without the presence of God in your life, you will live a powerless, defeated Christian life, without the ability to be a witness or do much in the kingdom of God. Demons do not fear one who is not holy (*perfect*).

Being perfect does not mean that we never do anything wrong, or commit any kind of sin. What is perfection then? It has to do with godly character and living a consecrated, righteous life before the Lord. "My servant Job...a perfect and upright man, one that fears God and avoids evil" *(Job 1:8)*.

Noah was declared also perfect by God in *Genesis 6:9*. Notice what it says: "Because Noah walked with God." Enoch was another one that was perfect before God because He walked with God *(Genesis 5:22)*. Daniel, Joseph, Abraham, Elijah and Elisha to name a few, lived lives of consecration (*perfection*) *(2 Corinthians 6:16, 7:1)*.

Our character will never rise above our level of obedience to the dealings of the Holy Spirit with each of us. When you make a mistake, admit it. Errors can be forgiven, but foolishness destroys character. David made a mistake but corrected it when confronted *(2 Samuel 19:1-8)*. Say the truth always, not half-truths. Half-truths are just as bad as a lie *(Proverbs 16:13)*.

Godly character involves living a life of transparency, humility and accountability to other people, not just to God. Our character will be formed by all the accumulated responses to the Holy Spirit's refining process in our life. This process will slowly form an inner value system, a grid of convictions and personal heart issues that will guide us throughout our lives. But in order for this to take place, we have to make ourselves available to the Holy Spirit to correct our wrong attitudes, understanding and perspective of truth, and spend much time in God's presence and His Word to receive a divine impartation of His character and presence in our lives.

C. Jesus Christ Your Example

He is our example in word and deed *(1 Corinthians 11:1; 1 Peter 2:21-24)*. We can walk as He walked and talk as He talked. But before we are able to walk and talk like He did, we must first begin to think as He thought *(Mark 7:21-23)*. The Bible says that a man becomes what he thinks in his heart *(Proverbs 23:7)*. To accomplish this we must bring into captivity every thought to the obedience of Christ *(2 Corinthians 10:5)*.

This doesn't just happen. It is an act of consecration, discipline, purpose and continual application because our mind loves to wander. What you say must correspond with what you do, and what you do must correspond with what you say. When you offer to do something, do it. Not doing it speaks of weakness of character *(Ecclesiastes 5:4; Proverbs 6:2)*. Words without actions are like clouds without water. Better not to promise, than promise and not do. Everything you do reflects character, because what you do is more important than what you say. Character is formed by actions, not words.

Our old way of thinking must be abandoned, and accept as our own the mind of Christ *(Phil. 2:5, 4:8)*. The evil suggestions of the enemy cannot be stopped from

71

entering our minds, but we do not have to dwell on it. We can drive them out by filling our minds with God thoughts *(I Peter 2:21-22, I John 3:6)*. We must walk in love and compassion for others even as Jesus did. His words were filled with power and authority *(Matthew 8:16)*. Our words can also be with power and authority if we endeavor to talk and walk as He did.

D. Deny Yourself

Jesus walked the path of self-denial. And if we desire to be imitators of Him, we must deny ourselves. Many lack the power of God in their lives because they never deny themselves any pleasure or desire their bodies crave. Most Christians pray very little and never fast. A disciple of Christ must make an effort, with the help of the Holy Spirit, to overcome the works of the flesh:

1. Uncleanness

This is what we could call immoderate desires, laziness and love of ease. In this nation, because of our permissive society, most Christians really struggle with this. We are just too spoiled.

2. Pride

The Bible says that God resists the proud, but gives grace to the humble *(1Peter 5:5)*. Pride manifests as self-importance, an independent spirit, stiffness, being demanding, boastful, love of praise, selfish, jealous, envious, and overbearing, love of being coaxed and humored, stubborn, and being un-teachable.

3. Strife

As a child of God, we should try to walk in peace with each other. Strife is the offspring of pride, and manifests itself as argumentative, quarrelsome, hatred, discord, contention, violent anger, rage, talkative, complaining, critical, nagging, fretting and unyielding.

4. Lust

The Bible talks about the lust of the eyes and the lust of the flesh *(1 John 2:16)*. Lust manifests itself as love of food, money, power, unholy actions, undue affection, familiarity towards opposite sex and wandering eyes.

5. Dishonesty

Dishonesty is what the world would call a liar. A person that manifests this trait is deceitful, distorts truth, manipulates facts, exaggerates and tries to leave an untrue impression of self.

6. Formality

This is another word for what we would call a religious spirit and legalism. It manifests as spiritual deadness, lack of love, mercy & compassion, dryness, indifference and lack of tolerance.

E. Take Up Your Cross & Follow Him

What is a cross? The burden of pain, sorrow and sacrifice which we could choose to lay aside, but instead carry willingly for the sake of others. It is that which in the natural we would lay aside. We didn't have to endure the cross. We must however take up the cross daily, willingly and carry it faithfully without fretting.

The world does not understand our cross, but each of us has our own God-appointed cross, whether we choose to bear it or not. It is not sickness, which we are helpless to lay aside. It is not unpleasant circumstances that we can do nothing about. It's that, which we accept willingly, at personal sacrifice to ourselves, in order to be obedient to God and bless others. When you take up your cross and follow Jesus Christ you are going to experience misunderstandings, unappreciated service, rejection, verbal and physical persecution, and in some countries, even death.

F. I Must Decrease & He Must Increase

You may call it self-respect, good breeding, poise, but Jesus calls it pride, and pride is a *sin*. We must come to realize our utter and total dependence upon God, and how little our own efforts are worth. Even our best efforts are futile. God must take full control of our life. But before that happens, our own personality, talents, knowledge and natural abilities must decrease in importance in our own eyes.

We must receive the revelation that the success of my life and ministry depends upon the amount or greatness of God in my life. It is only when self decreases in us that He starts to increase in us. The measure of how much God increases in us is proportional to how much self decreases in us. We have to decrease and He must increase in us, as we come to understand that without God, we are nothing!

If you are interested in more information about our ministry, and obtaining some of our materials, books and Music CD's please visit our website at: www.theappearance.com *or you may write to us at:*

Augusto Perez
PO Box 465
Live Oak, FL. 32064

www.ingramcontent.com/pod-product-compliance
Lightning Source LLC
Chambersburg PA
CBHW071841020426
42331CB00007B/1804